SONG
of the
SON OF MAN

From the First Noel to Ascension

DR. ELIZABETH NEWELL BERGLUND

WESTBOW
PRESS
A DIVISION OF THOMAS NELSON

WestBow Press books may be ordered through booksellers or by contacting:

WestBow Press
A Division of Thomas Nelson
1663 Liberty Drive
Bloomington, IN 47403
www.westbowpress.com
1-(866) 928-1240

Because of the dynamic nature of the Internet, any web addresses or
links contained in this book may have changed since publication and
may no longer be valid. The views expressed in this work are solely those
of the author and do not necessarily reflect the views of the publisher,
and the publisher hereby disclaims any responsibility for them.

Any people depicted in stock imagery provided by Thinkstock are models,
and such images are being used for illustrative purposes only.

Certain stock imagery © Thinkstock.

ISBN: 978-1-4908-0341-8 (sc)

Library of Congress Control Number: 2013913457

Printed in the United States of America.

WestBow Press rev. date: 9/19/2013

This book is dedicated to my daughter
BETTY WALTON
and to the loving memory of my parents
OLIVER LOWELL NEWELL
and
EDNA HAWKES NEWELL

FOREWORD

From the time of my earliest childhood I've always been sure that there was a God. I could feel it in the air as I breathed. As I remember running in the wind and having my hair blow. It was like a caress of God. To me in the Spring I could hear God's voice in the peeping of the frogs. In the Summer His face was in every flower and in the Fall I could hear his Whisper as I ran through the rows of tall growing corn. In the Winter the silence of a snowy night and pictures on the window glass in the morning revealed a wonderful drama—the caring gift of God.

You might easily say, "Why write poetry from the biblical passages? Aren't the passages alone, good enough?" Of course that is the case, but poetry is the joyous celebration of that which is close to our heart. I remember the thought came to me twenty years ago, when with a heart full of pain, I walked down the streets of Lexington. It was at noon as I heard the bells of the church playing the hymn "What a Friend We Have In Jesus," and the thought was very comforting. I believe it was at that moment that the <u>Song of the Son of Man</u> began to grow in my heart.

The song has grown stronger and more meaningful with study during the years which have followed, and have taken me from the time of the Annunciation through the Nativity, His years of preparation, His ministry, through the Passion and Resurrection and finally the echo of His song around the world.

Table of Contents

PRELUDE

Part I
The First Noel

Part II
The Birth of a Ministry

BOOK II

BOOK III

Part I
PREPARATION FOR PASSOVER

Part II
MAUNDY THURSDAY

Part III
ARREST AND TRIAL

Part IV
CRUCIFIXION AND RESURRECTION

Part V

Part VI
POSTLUDE

PRELUDE

I

THE ANNUNCIATION

At a time when she was alone came the visitation
Of God's own angel and Mary of Galilee,
Sounding the wondrous words of Annunciation.
"Hail! Oh favored one, the Lord is with thee."
And she answered, "I'm only a maiden of Nazareth."
"You are God's own chosen one," said Gabriel.
"And think of your elderly cousin, Elisabeth,
Who will soon bear a son through a miracle.
Indeed! You are even more blessed than she, for I tell
You, the Holy Spirit will come to you,
And your son will be acclaimed Emmanuel."
Then the angel slowly faded from Mary's view,
       While she bowed her head and whispered, reverently,
       "May the will of God, then be fulfilled in me."

II

SONG OF PRAISE

Still pondering the news of the messenger
Of God, then Mary knew she must visit the childless
Home of her cousin where the angel ambassador
Had promised the birth of a son to Zacharias
And his wife, well advanced in years. When Mary greeted
Her cousin, who then was filled with the Holy Spirit,
Elisabeth cried out, "Oh, Mary, most blessed
Of women! A son will be born to you, a celibate
Maiden! When I heard the sound of your voice in greeting
The baby within me jumped in joyfulness!"
With outstretched arms, and a heart filled with knowing,
Mary stood transfixed in blessedness,
> While she answered in joyous song of praise for the Godsend
> Of the Holy Spirit, and the kingdom with no end.

PART I

THE NEW NOEL

III

JERUSALEM, THE JEWEL

The fatigue of the five day's journey to Bethlehem
Had dulled the senses of Mary on the donkey's back,
When at once she heard Joseph exclaim, "Jerusalem!"
And all of her weariness faded as wonderstruck,
From Olivet they gazed at the great stone wall
Surrounding the precious glory of the Holy City,
Where the glow of the sun at even-fall
Highlighted their view from across the Kidron valley.
In a spiritual ecstasy of marveling
At the city and all they knew of its history,
They conversed in duet as in wondrous song to be sung,
Until Joseph turned to Mary when suddenly he asked,
    "Are you feeling pain? There's no cause for fright."
    She answered, "The baby will be born tonight."

IV

ONWARD TO BETHLEHEM

Mary settled again on the donkey as Joseph started
To lead the way around the city wall,
And through the Hinnom Valley to the City of David.
It now seemed as if the land lay vertical,
With the road to Bethlehem a steady climb,
And filled with travelers, some even sleeping
By the roadside. Though feeling pain, Mary hoped there was
Time to reach the high and distant cliff overlooking
The valley. When at last they reached the long sought inn,
Joseph went inside, assuring his wife
Of immediate lodging, but he soon returned in chagrin
With the offer of a manger in which to welcome new life.
    "Take me there," said Mary, "for my time is near.
    This is the will of God. We'll have no fear."

V

IN A MANGER BORN

Joseph led the donkey with its precious burden
Down the cliff to the entrance of the cattle cave
Where at last Mary slid down to the ground, and then
She noted the livestock sheltered there that eve.
Joseph lit a stable lantern hanging
On a peg nearby, with the cattle watching curiously
As he prepared the empty stall with a filling
Of straw before looking around for water in the shadowy
Manger. When he'd made a fire outside for the heating
Of water, he then went out at Mary's request.
And watched a distant star over the mountain rising,
Until he heard a tiny cry at last.
    When Mary called to him on that early morn.
    And he went inside to kneel beside the newly born.

VI

THE SHEPHERDS WORSHIP

In a valley near Bethlehem some shepherds were watching
Their sheep at night when the sky was filled with a light
Like the noonday sun, and some of the shepherds who were
Sleeping awakened in fear to see the sky so bright.
Then an angel appeared to them over the valley,
And the shepherds studied the sky with sober brown
Eyes as the angel spoke, "I bring news of great joy:
A savior was born tonight in David's town."
In a moment the angel was joined by others singing,
"Glory to God in the highest, and on earth peace,
And good will to men. You will find the baby lying
In a manger." And marveling at the chosen birthplace,
    The shepherds went to visit the newborn king,
    His first disciples in their worshiping.

VII

VISIT OF THE MAGI

On the night of the birth in the manger, the blue-white star
Which appeared over Bethlehem was seen by many,
And studied by three philosophers from afar
In the east, who saw it as fulfillment of prophesy,
Through the birth of the King of Kings. They set out on a journey
At night with the brilliance of the star guiding them
To Jerusalem, where their unusual inquiry
Brought response from Herod. "That we may worship Him,
Bring us word from Bethlehem when your mission
Is complete," he said. But his word did not deter
The wise men who honored the newborn Nazarene
With their gifts of gold, frankincense and myrrh.
　　And being warned in a dream of a plot by Herod,
　　They returned to their country by another road.

VIII

PRESENTATION IN JERUSALEM

In forty-one days came the time of Presentation
Of Jesus at the Temple in Jerusalem, and they prepared
As well for the ceremony of Purification
Of Mary, as required by law, in the temple of the Lord.
Now in Jerusalem was a God-fearing man
Whose name was Simeon, who'd received a promise
From the Holy Spirit that he would look upon
The Messiah before he died, and because of this
He'd attended the presentation every morning
For many years. When he peered at Jesus, of a sudden
The baby was in his arms: his time of waiting
Was over! With his eyes to the skies he crooned a hymn,
 "Oh, Lord," I go in peace, for now I have seen
 The promised light which you have caused to shine."

IX

FLIGHT TO EGYPT

On the morning following the ceremony
Of presentation, Joseph was awakened early
By and angel who warned him of approaching jeopardy.
"Rise," the angel gently commanded, "and flee
With your family into the land of Egypt on behalf
Of your child, for Herod will order his men to be searching
Everywhere for the baby in order that His life
May be taken. You'll remain in Egypt until the king
No longer remains a threat, and I will tell
You when that time has come." Then carefully
They prepared for the journey, and though they'd hoped
To dwell in Nazareth, they accepted the angel's decree.

    But Joseph pondered while the white-stoned path he trod,
    "How could one wish to kill the Son of God?"

X

LIKE RACHEL, THEY WEPT FOR THEIR CHILDREN

At his palace King Herod the Great was in a rage
As he spat out words to his men who stood around him.
The Magi had returned to the east from their pilgrimage,
And had failed to report their news in the interim.
"The census," he roared, "This is where we'll begin
To solve the problem!" And he ordered the soldiers to seek
A list of all near Bethlehem with a son
Two years of age or less, and ordered the soldiers to kill
The babies so listed. The slaughter of the innocent
Began, as young boys were snatched from their domicile
In accordance with orders none dared to circumvent.

    And the elders recalled the words of a prophet of yore,
    "Rachel wept for her children who were no more."

XI

RETURN TO NAZARETH

When the Holy family had lived in Egypt for a time
Joseph was awakened by another visitation.
"Rise," the angel said, "and go to your home
In Nazareth, for the cause of trepidation
In Jerusalem is dead," When Joseph told Mary
The news they began their journey across the desert
Toward their homeland, plodding relentlessly,
Until word from travelers caused them to skirt
The Holy City, where it was known that the son
Of Herod was now on the throne; if their child should be seen
When others of his age had been killed, then someone
Would report the fact to the king, and this could mean
    Disaster; so they changed their route and went to their home
    In Nazareth, and the blessing of God was with them.

XII

BOY OF TWELVE

For six weeks now, Jesus had been preparing
With his parents for the Festival of Passover,
Its story and meaning the subject of daily teaching
In the synagogue in all its traditional splendor.
To a very young boy of twelve, this was a day
Of days when his parents joined the caravan for the journey
To Jerusalem, with plenty of time on the way
To remember the time when God had mercifully
Delivered his people. As they neared their destination
The expectation of Jesus was kindled the greater
When he glimpsed the Holy City from across the Lidron
And was touched by a sudden difference in the atmosphere:

> The many miles they had traveled were wearisome,
> Why did He feel as if He had now reached home?

XIII

IN HIS FATHER'S HOUSE

The mind of young Jesus was filled with expectation
As He climbed Mount Zion with the heavy traffic flow
Of those who were singing the song of many a generation
Of Passover Pilgrims, "I was glad when they said, 'Let me go
To the house of the Lord!'" However, when He later
Went with Joseph to the temple court, where the sanctified
Lamb was slain, Jesus began to wonder
How all of that blood could bring one closer to God.
But there still was hope . . . He would go to the Jewish court,
The Great Sanhedrin, embodying the highest
Wisdom. In the temple, three days later when found apart
From His family who spoke to Him of being distressed,

> He answered, "Why did you need to look for me further,
> Didn't you know I'd be in the House of my Father?"

PART II

BIRTH OF A MINISTRY

XIV

FORERUNNER, JOHN THE BAPTIST

It was during the rule of Tiberius, with Pontius
Pilate serving as Governor of Judea,
When God's Spirit spoke to the son of Zacharias,
And John answered by beginning to preach
"God's Kingdom is near."
The Jews sent priests and Levites out to him
From Jerusalem, "Tell us! Who are you? They asked.
"I'm surely not the Messiah," John answered them.
"Are you Elijah, or one of the prophets promised?"
And John then said, "I'm the voice of one crying
In the wilderness. I came this way to induce
The people to Baptism, but another one is coming
Whose sandals I'm most unworthy to unloose.

    To baptize with water, my way does most befit,
    But He is prepared to baptize with the Holy Spirit."

XV

THE BAPTISM OF JESUS

Then Jesus went to the Jordan from Galilee
To be baptized by John, but as he drew
Near, John exclaimed, "You come to me
When it's I who ought to be baptized by you?"
And Jesus answered him, "Let it be for now,
For in this we know we are only doing God's will."
So John agreed, and when all had taken their vow,
He turned to Jesus, His baptismal wish to fulfill.
And while Jesus lost Himself in deepest praying,
The heavens opened, and the Holy Spirit descended
Upon Him like a dove, while a voice from heaven was saying,
"My own beloved Son in whom I am well pleased."
    And Jesus knew His work had now begun,
    As He also knew that He was God's own Son.

XVI

JESUS IN THE WILDERNESS

God's Spirit then led Jesus into the desert,
Where He lived for forty days, eating nothing.
And though He was nearly famished, He remained alert
When approached by the devil, persistent in his testing.
"If you're God's son, then turn this stone into
A loaf of bread," he said. And Jesus answered
"Life is more than food. The spirit also
Must be fed." But the devil was undeterred,
And Jesus was taken to Jerusalem and the highest
Ledge of the temple and told to jump which He
Refused, as well as the devil's final test,
"The world is yours, if you bend your knee to me."
    The tempter then went his way to other deeds
    While angels ministered to Jesus' needs.

XVII

LAMB OF GOD

When Jesus finally from the desert was emerging,
He went again to the Jordan where its habitué
Was baptizing and preaching, and when He was seen
John said, "Here's the Lamb of God who takes away
The sin of the world." And then in testimony
He continued, "It is He, of whom I said, from the throne
Of God there is one who is coming after me,
And I have come before Him to make Him known
To Israel. I saw the Spirit coming
Down on Him, and God's words were definite,
'The One on whom you see the Light descending
Is the chosen one, who is filled with the Holy Spirit.'

    I saw it happen, this sign of heaven's own rod:
    My witness stands. This man is the Son of God!"

XVIII

FIRST DISCIPLES

On the very next day when John was standing with two
Of his disciples, it happened that Jesus was walking
By, and John said to them. "There goes the true
Lamb of God. And, later when they were following
Jesus, He turned to the two by His side asking
"Are you looking for someone?" They answered Him,
"Where do you live, Rabbi?" And Jesus replied,
"Come and see." So they spent the remaining time
In that day with Him. One of the men was Andrew
Who later found his brother Simon and exclaimed,
"Come with me! I think we have found the Messiah!"
And they went to Jesus who looked at the brother and said,

'You are Simon, son of John, but in my flock
You'll be known as Cephas, or Peter, which means a rock."

XIX

WEDDING AT CANA

On the following day when Jesus was attending a wedding
At Cana in the highlands of Galilee with his newly
Designated disciples also accompanying
Him, His mother, who was present at the ceremony,
Discovered they had run out of wine and came to Him
And said, "We are out of wine!" And Jesus answered,
"You must not tell me what to do, for my time
Has not yet come." But His mother was not deterred
From instructing the servants to do as Jesus requested.
And when asked to fill the jars with water, they did
So at once. Later, when it was passed out and tasted
It was found that the water had turned to wine indeed!

    Thus, Jesus performed His initial mighty deed
      Which began His work, even as a mustard seed.

XX

NICODEMUS

After the wedding in Cana, Jesus' stay
In Capernaum was brief, for the solemn time
Of Passover was near, and He went away
To Jerusalem, where a man from the noble Sanhedrin,
Nicodemus, came to visit Him
At night and said, "Rabbi, we know you're a teacher
Come from God. "And Jesus answered, "The Kingdom
Is seen by those who are born anew, since they enter
Through the birth of the Spirit." "But how can that be?"
And His answer came, "It's like the wind that blows
Wherever it wishes: though we hear, we cannot see
From whence it comes, and we know not where it goes.

    The spiritual birth is like the winds that blow,
    The coming and going is for God alone to know."

XXI

JOHN IS SENT TO PRISON

Then Jesus went to the province of Judea
With His disciples, and spent some time with them
In His teaching. And at that time John was also
Performing rites in Aenon, not far from Salim.
When some of John's disciples spoke to him
Of many who were going to Jesus, John reminded
Them, "I'm not the Messiah, but I have come
Ahead of Him with a message, serving as prelude
To what He was sent to say. The One from God
Speaks with fullness of spirit, as His only Son."
Later, when John spoke out against King Herod
And his evil ways, he was quickly sent to prison.
    And when Jesus heard that John had been taken away,
    He left Judea, and traveled to Galilee.

XXII

THE SAMARITAN AT THE WELL

When John was in prison, and Jesus was on His way
To Galilee, He came to a town called Sychar,
Where He stopped at Jacob's well at noon that day.
And as He sat to rest near a very large water jar.
He asked a Samaritan woman standing nearby,
"Would you give me water, please?" His disciples had
Gone into town to buy some food. The woman's reply
Was immediate. "As a jew, do you not disdain
To use this vessel?" And Jesus answered her,
"Those who drink this water will be thirsty
Again, but the water I give is living water,
And will spring within you, throughout eternity."
   Then she answered, "The Messiah will tell us what to do."
   And Jesus said, "He is talking now to you."

XXIII

HEALING OF THE GOVERNMENT OFFICIAL'S SON

In Galilee then Jesus found that He
Was welcomed by all of the people, for they had gone
To the Passover Feast, and were privileged to see
In Jerusalem some deeds which He had done
While there. Now when He entered the town of Cana,
In Galilee where He'd turned the water into
Wine, He met an official nearing hysteria
Because of his son in Capernaum who he knew
Was about to die. He asked Jesus to remedy
The illness which would surely take him away.
And Jesus said, "They believe if they can see,
Now go to him! Your son will live today."

On the official's homeward journey came news which relieved
His fears: his son would live, and he believed.

XXIV

THE HEALING OF PETER'S MOTHER-IN-LAW

After a service in the synagogue one day,
Jesus was invited to the home of Simon and Andrew.
James and John had also been asked to stay.
Now when Jesus arrived, He found that Peter's mother-in-law
Had become very ill. When Jesus went to her side
And took her by the hands to help her up
She began to move about and prepared the food
For all of those who met in fellowship.
As the sun was setting that day, a crowd had gathered
Outside the house. It seemed that everyone
Having a relative or friend with health impaired
Had come. When Jesus appeared amidst the din
    A silence fell and all eyes were fixed upon Him
    As He touched the head of each in healing them.

XXV

TEACHING, PREACHING AND HEALING IN GALILEE

Early in the morning, before it was daylight,
Jesus left Peter's home and went to a lonely
Place to pray, but Peter and the others went out
To look for Him. They spoke impetuously
When they found Him, "Everyone is looking for you."
And Jesus answered, "We must go to other
Towns, for I must preach to them anew
Because that is why I came." And He went all over
Galilee preaching Good News of the Kingdom,
Teaching the people in their synagogue, and healing
Them from every kind of troublesome
Affliction, until large crowds were following,
 Not only from Galilee, but from every town
 From Jerusalem to lands lying east of the Jordan.

XXVI

A LARGE CATCH OF FISH

While Jesus was standing near Lake Gennesaret
The people gathered close to Him to listen
To the word of God, and when He saw a boat
On the beach which He recognized as belonging to Simon
He stepped inside and asked to be pushed off shore
Where He sat in the boat and continued to teach the throng;
And when He'd finished, He said, "Now push out further
For a catch." Then Peter answered, "All night long
We fished these waters without a catch, but I'll
Let down the nets again as you say." When they let
The nets down again they were filled in a very short while,
And all were amazed at the number of fish they had caught.
    Then Peter exclaimed, "Oh Master, I'm filled with sin."
    And Jesus answered, "You'll soon be catching men."

XXVII

REJECTED AT NAZARETH

Then Jesus traveled to the town where He'd been reared,
And on the Sabbath Day, He went as usual
To the synagogue; and when He stood to read
From the book which He'd been given, He unrolled the scroll
Of Isaiah and began, "The Spirit of the Lord is upon
Me, for He has chosen me to preach the Good News
With an understanding of the Kingdom of God as the keystone
To the way of all liberty and freedom, because
Of God's own promise." As He finished the reading,
All eyes were fixed upon Him as He said, "This passage
Has come true today!" There was silence . . . and then
everything
Was in upheaval, while Jesus in the midst of the rampage,
    Slipped away from Nazareth, which He held dear,
    But still He preached, "The Kingdom of Heaven is near."

XXVIII

HEALING OF THE PARALYZED MAN

One day when Jesus was teaching those who were sitting
Before Him from many towns from miles away,
And the power of God was present in Him for healing,
Some men who carried a paralyzed man who lay
On a bed were trying their best to allow the suffering
One to come before Him, but could find no way
Until on the roof they made an opening
And lowered the man to the middle of the group that day.
When Jesus saw the extent of their faith, He said,
"Your sins are forgiven!" And the man stood up and began
To walk. But some officers thought such power was attributed
Only to God. And Jesus said to the man,

"I will prove to you that the Son of Man
Has authority on earth to forgive all sin."

XXIX

A HEALING AT
THE BETHESDA POOL

Then came the time of one of the Jewish religious
Feasts when Jesus traveled to the Holy City and passed
Through the gate near the pool with its own five porches,
Known as Bethesda, the house of grace and gratuity.
On all of the porches were lying those who were ill;
The blind, the lame, and the paralyzed. With intensity,
All were waiting for the water to be stirred by an angel
Of the Lord, believed to come occasionally
To ripple its surface. When Jesus looked at a man
Who was lying there, He said, "Do you wish to get well?"
And the paralyzed man then answered Him, "I can
If I reach the pool when the water is stirring." "I tell
    You now," said Jesus, "Pick up your mat and walk."
    And he did, while authorities began their talk.

XXX

QUESTION OF THE SABBATH

Since the day was a Sabbath, the authorities said to the grateful
Man who was healed at the pool, "It's against our Law
For you to carry your mat on a Sabbath. Tell
Us then, who is this man, this mysterious visitor
With the healing power?" Now Jesus had slipped away
Into the crowd, and the man did not know who
Had accomplished the healing until he heard the Lord say,
"Repent, and nothing more will happen to you."
And when Jesus was identified with the miracle healing
They began to persecute Him because it was done
On a Sabbath Day. But Jesus said, "I am doing
Only as God has instructed the Son of Man."

But He knew the intent of many a Pharisee
And He withdrew once again to Galilee.

XXXI

CHOOSING HIS TWELVE

In Galilee then Jesus went to a nearby
Mountain spot where He spent the night in prayer
And when it was day, He elected to identify
A selection of twelve apostles who would minister
To others all of His teachings: there was Simon, called Peter,
And Andrew, his brother who came from near the sea
Of Galilee; and then those "Sons of Thunder,"
James and John, the sons of Zebedee.
There was Thomas, The twin and Philip of Bethsaida,
Mathew, Simon, and James the son of Alphaeus,
And Nathanael, thought to have been at Cana,
And Judas, sometimes known as Thaddaeus,
      And lastly Judas Iscariot to be
      Remembered always for betrayal at Gethsemane.

XXXII

FIRST DAY WITH HIS TWELVE

As Jesus walked by the sea with His chosen men
While healing the ill in Capernaum that day,
He knew it was time for Him to be alone
With His Twelve, that instruction proceed without delay.
When the press of the people grew greater at sundown, He sought
A fisherman's boat, and the thirteen sailed out of sight
Of the crowds and beached at a desolate spot on the opposite
Side of the sea near a mountain of towering height.
It was there that they climbed a path, well known to Jesus,
Until high on the mount, in a space overlooking the shore
They stood on a sheltered ledge, impervious
To the night as they joined in a circle of silent prayer,
    While the star-lit beams on the waters of Galilee,
    Were merged with the radiance of eternity.

SONG OF THE SON OF MAN

The Ministry of Jesus Christ

BOOK II
OF A
TRILOGY

I

SERMON ON THE MOUNT

On the mount a crowd had gathered as Jesus began
To teach. "Blessed are the poor, for yours is the Kingdom
Of God. Blessed are you who hunger when
You know you'll be satisfied. Your time will come
To laugh if you have wept. Rejoice in the day
Your name is excluded on account of the Son of Man,
For the same was done to the prophets. Leap for joy,
For behold! Your reward is always great in heaven.
Love your enemies, and do good to those who hate you.
Bless those who abuse you, and for those who curse you, pray,
And give to those who would even take away;
As you wish that men should do to you, do so
    To them, for the children of God are kind to the ungrateful,
    And are merciful, even as your Father is merciful."

II

ABOUT PRAYER

When Jesus' disciples asked Him how to pray,
He said, "Be not like a hypocrite who is sure
To pray in a place where everyone can see;
But remember to go to your room and close the door,
And pray to your Father who is also unseen,
And He will see you in private and answer you.
Now, since your Father knows your needs, you'll refrain
From lengthy prayer, and these are the words you'll say:
'Our Father in heaven, may your Holy Name be honored;
May your Kingdom come on earth, as it is in Heaven,
Let us know this day that our bread shall be assured,
And forgive us our debts, as we forgive everyone
 Indebted to us, and deliver us from temptation,
 For thine is the power, and the glory forever, Amen.'"

III

HEALING THE CENTURIAN'S SERVANT

When Jesus had finished saying these things, He went
Away to Capernaum, and while He was there
A kindly Roman officer then sent
Some elders to ask for the healing of a servant who was dear
To him. "This man deserves your help," they said.
"He loves our people, and it was he who built
Our beautiful synagogue." So Jesus did
As asked, but near the house where the officer dwelt
He was met by friends of the officer to tell
Of his request, "I'm most unworthy for you to come in person,
But please give your order to make my servant well
Then Jesus turned to speak of what He had seen,

    "This man who walks in His everlasting faith,
    Shall never know the pain which comes with death."

IV

JESUS ON TOUR

It was at this time that Jesus went on a preaching
Tour throughout the towns of Galilee
Teaching good news of the Kingdom. And traveling
With His twelve, were some women in His coterie
Who were grateful to Him for His healings. One of the women
In the group was Mary, called Mary Magdalene,
Who was filled with gratitude to be free from the seven
Demons cast out from her by Jesus, and again
A woman known as Joanna, wife of Chusa,
An agent of Herod's. and several others who
Cared for the needs of the traveling company
By using their personal funds most willingly;
    For among the supporters of a cause have always been
    Individuals who chose to remain unsung and unseen.

V

A WOMAN WASHES JESUS' FEET

When Jesus was with Simon the Pharisee,
A woman who lived a sinful life became
Aware that Jesus was in the territory,
So she brought an alabaster jar of perfume,
And stood by Jesus' side crying and wetting
His feet with her tears, and then she began to dry them
With her hair, after pouring perfume. And Simon was thinking,
"If this man is a prophet, He will know that touching Him
Is a sinful woman." Then Jesus stood and said,
"Two men owed money, one owed fifty and the other
Five hundred. When debts were cancelled, which love then
Measured more?" Came the answer, "The one forgiven more."
    "Correct! Great love bespeaks forgiveness," said Jesus,
        And He turned to the woman, "Go in your faith and peace."

VI

WHY PARABLES?

One day when Jesus was teaching by Lake Galilee
His disciples came to Him and asked, "Why
Do you speak in parables to them?" And He
Answered, "Knowledge of God's Kingdom was given to you,
But not to them. They look but do not see,
And they listen, but they do not hear, or understand,
In this case the prophesy of Isaiah comes true;
They have truly blocked the pathway to the mind.
As for you, how very fortunate you are!
Your eyes are able to see, and your ears are free
To hear, but many of God's people wanted to hear,
And even some of the prophets with poignancy,

    Have longed to see for themselves what you have seen,
    And to truly understand what you have known!"

VII

PARABLE OF THE SOWER

Then Jesus told them a parable, "The Kingdom
Of Heaven is like the man who sowed good seed
In his field, but when all were asleep an enemy came
And walked among the wheat to plant some weeds,
And went away. The plants were quick to grow,
With heads of grain appearing on the wheat,
But among the grain some weeds began to show.
And his servants said to him, 'Your fields are replete
With weeds! You planted good seeds, how could this be?'
And he answered, 'It all was done by an enemy.'
'Do you wish us to pull the weeds?' they inquired.
He answered, 'At harvest we'll take the weeds and tie
    Them in bundles, for casting into the fire to burn,
    Then gather the wheat and put it in my barn.'"

VIII

AS A MUSTARD SEED

And Jesus began to speak to them again
In another parable. "The Kingdom of God
Is as if a man should scatter seeds upon
The ground, and then he will go his way, and the seeds
Will sprout and grow until harvest. With what can we
Compare the Kingdom of God? It is like a grain
Of mustard seed, the smallest of seeds to sow,
Yet, when this diminutive seed is sown,
It grows until of all the shrubs, it becomes the greatest,
With its spreading branches beckoning birds of the air
To come and build their homes in this friendliest
Of shades, where they find a safe and welcome harbor.

    For God alone brings in the Kingdom, but we know
    We must make the conditions in which the seeds will grow.

IX

HEALING OF JAIRUS' DAUGHTER

When Jesus went back to the other side of the sea
A very large crowd had gathered around Jairus,
An official of the synagogue who was filled with worry
When he came to Jesus and said, "Your miraculous
Deeds are well known. My daughter is ill.
Please come and place your hands on her for we know
You have special power which can make her whole
Again and remove the threat of this death blow."
Then Jesus went to the home with the father and mother
And He entered the room where their endangered daughter was.
He took the child by the hand and said to her,
"Little girl, get up!" And she did and started walking.
    All were completely amazed at what He had done,
    But Jesus gave orders for them to tell no one.

X

JESUS COMMISSIONS
HIS APOSTLES

Jesus called His apostles together, and when
He'd vested them with power and authority
To cure disease, and to cast out demons, He began
To instruct them concerning their work in the territory.
"Remember to stay away from Samaria,
Seek instead the lost sheep of Israel.
Go and preach that the Kingdom of God is nearby.
Drive out demons, make lepers clean, and heal
The sick. You've received without pay so give without pay,
Carry nothing, and the Spirit of the Father will be speaking
Whenever you say in greeting. 'Peace be with you!'"
Be cautious, but gentle in all of your preaching and teaching.
    It will not be easy to preach the glory of God's Kingdom,
    But the day of the Son of Man will surely come!"

XI

FEEDING THE FIVE THOUSAND

The apostles returned from their tour and met with the Master
To tell Him all they had done and taught, but many
Who wished to hear the words of Jesus drew near
Until Jesus said, "On the other side of the sea
We will rest awhile." So they went in a boat across to a lonely
Place, but the people ran ahead by land
To be with them, and Jesus was filled with pity,
For they seemed like sheep without a shepherd.
He bade five thousand to sit on the grass as He broke
The bread and gave thanks to God, and rejoicingly
They shared five loaves and two fishes with all to partake,
And plenty for everyone. When they saw the mighty
    Work of Jesus, they claimed Him the awaited Messiah,
    But He slipped away to the mountains alone to pray.

XII

JESUS, "THE BREAD OF LIFE"

On the following day when the people were looking for Him
Again, then Jesus said, "It's because of the food . . .
You ate the bread and were given every crumb
You wanted. It's not because you understand
My practice of power. You must work for food to abide
In eternal life, the food which the Son of Man
Will give to you, because the Father has honored
My work." And the people gathered around Him and began
With the question, "How can we prepare to do
God's work?" And Jesus answered, "To believe in the One
He sent comes first in the mission which God asks of you,
For the bread which is given to you comes down from Heaven,
　　And gives life to the world. I am the Bread of Life
　　Which God has sent to you on His behalf."

XIII

JESUS RECEIVES NEWS
OF JOHN'S DEATH

In Jerusalem when the news of Jesus' healing
Reached Herod, he said, "Is it John come back to life?"
The very man he had put to death for saying,
"It's not right for you to marry your brother's wife."
Now Herod's wife had held a grudge against John,
And wanted to kill him. But Herod was afraid, for he knew
That John was a holy man in close commune
With God, and he liked to listen to him, although
He usually became disturbed by his talk. Finally,
The daughter, Salome, had danced on Herod's birthday
And received John's head on a platter accordingly
As pawn, her mother's hate to satisfy.
    Jesus was stunned by the news too odious
    For belief, but He knew of the darkness in Herodias

XIV

A SYROPHOENECIAN WOMAM'S DAUGHTER IS HEALED

Then Jesus left Galilee and went away
To Tyre, where a Syrophoenician woman came,
And knelt before Him. "Son of David, woe
Is upon me!" she cried. "Remove the demon from
My daughter!" and Jesus said, "But surely you know
That first of all the children must eat their fill.
We cannot take what belongs to them and throw
It out to feed the dogs." "But the crumbs which fall
Beneath the Master's table are eaten, even
By dogs, Oh Lord," she said. And He answered her,
"Because of your faith, your request is granted, woman.
Now go your way. The demon has left your daughter."

    And His words were echoing, "God's will be done,
    Let all of His children speak to Him as one."

XV

PETER'S DECLARATION

Then Jesus went to Caesarea Philippi
Alone, and when His apostles came to Him,
He put a burning question to them, "Who
Do the people say I am?" And they answered, "Some
Say, John the Baptist, while others say Elijah,
Or some of the other prophets." "And what about you?"
He asked, as He studied their faces carefully.
And Simon Peter said, "You are the Messiah,
Son of the living God." And Jesus answered
Him, "Blessed are you Simon, son
Of John, for flesh and blood has not revealed
To you a truth which comes from my Father in Heaven,
 You are Peter, and on this rock I'll build
 My church, and around it no soil will be left untilled."

XVI

JESUS INSTRUCTS THE DISCIPLES

From the very day of Peter's declaration,
The apostles were taught by Jesus that the Son of Man
Must suffer in order to build the church foundation
Which he'd described to them. But Peter began
To rebuke Him, "Lord," he said, "this must never
Happen to you!" But Jesus turned and said,
"Then you are an obstacle to me, Peter,
For yours are the thoughts of men, and not of God."
And He went on, "If anyone wants to come
With me, he will take up his cross and follow me,
For he who saves his life can lose the Kingdom,
While some who lose it will live eternally.
    For it's true that some of you who now are here
    Will see the Kingdom of God as it draws near.

XVII

THE TRANSFIGURATION

On the seventh day after Peter's witnessing,
Then Jesus led Peter, James and John to a site
On the top of a hill to pray. And while He was praying,
His appearance changed and His raiment became dazzling white.
And behold! It was Moses and Elijah who appeared in glory,
And spoke of Jesus' departure which soon would happen
In Jerusalem. Now Peter and the others were heavy
With sleep, and when they awakened, they saw the men
Who stood with Jesus in glory, and there came
A cloud, and out of that covering a voice was saying,
"This is my only Son! Listen to Him." And when
They came down from the mountains, Jesus was instructing
Them, "You will tell of this vision to no one," He said,
"Until the Son of Man is raised from the dead."

XVIII

FORGIVING ONE'S BROTHER

It all began with a question to Jesus from Peter,
"If my brother sins against me, and is then forgiven
Seven times, is that enough?" "Never,"
Said Jesus, "It is more than seventy times seven.
The Kingdom of Heaven is like the story of a king
Who forgave a servant a very large sum of money,
And when that man went out and met one owing
Him only several drachmas, he relentlessly
Demanded payment, with no propensity
For leniency. Now, when his master knew
Of this, he said, 'You should have shown more mercy
For a fellow servant, as I had mercy on you.

    You must now be punished,'" Jesus said, "My Father
    Will view you the same, if you fail to forgive your brother."

XIX

AT THE FEAST OF TABERNACLES

At the time when the Feast of Tabernacles was being
Celebrated in Jerusalem, it was known
By the residents that Jesus would be arriving
And He became the topic of conversation.
On the final day of the feast, Jesus
Stood up in the temple and asked, "Is anyone thirsty?
Let him come to me and drink and just as the scriptures
Say, living water will spring within you."
He referred to the gift of the Holy Spirit to be given
To those who believed in Him when He returned to heaven.
But His teaching divided the crowd and they began
To argue, "Surely this man is the Christ." And then
Came a voice, "Go read the scriptures and you will see.
That the Christ will never come from Galilee."

XX

A WOMAN CAUGHT IN ADULTERY

After spending the night on the Mount of Olives, early
The next morning Jesus went back to the temple
Where a woman caught in the act of committing adultery
Was brought before Him. "Teacher," they said, "this example
Under the Law of Moses indicates that such
A woman be stoned to death. What do you say?"
Jesus was silent, and then he bent to touch
His fingers to the ground where he allowed the sand to convey
His thoughts while all were watching, then finally
He said, "Whoever has committed no sin may throw
The first stone." And He bent again to write in mystery
As slowly from the oldest to the youngest He heard them go
    And Jesus and the woman were alone, standing there
    And He said, "Freely go and sin no more!"

XXI

TO KNOW THE TRUTH

At festival time when Jesus was teaching anew
In the temple, He spoke of abiding loyalty.
"Continue in my word," He said, "Then you
Will know the truth, and the truth shall make you free."
"But we are Abraham's children," His listeners cried,
"And have never been in bondage to any one!"
"A sinner is a slave of sin," then Jesus replied,
"But in Abraham, I find no comparison."
"So you have seen him? And you are not yet fifty!"
They scoffed. And Jesus answered, "Abraham,
Your father, rejoiced that he would surely see
My day, for before Abraham was, I am."
⠀⠀⠀The crowd then took up stones to throw at Him.
⠀⠀⠀But He slipped away from the temple avoiding them.

XXII

A BLIND MAN HEALED

As Jesus left the temple, He passed a man
Made blind from his birth, and His disciples asked,
"Was it this man or his parents who committed a sin?"
"It was neither the man, nor his parents," Jesus declared.
"It was sent that God's work be manifest in him,
And I must do that work while it still is day,
For the night will soon be with us; while here I am
The light of the world!" Then he spat on the ground and
made clay
Of His spittle and anointed the eyes of the man, saying,
"Go quickly now, and wash in the Pool of Siloam!"
The man went where he was sent and came back seeing,
And he looked around as he called out Jesus' name,
    But the Master had done His work, and had gone His way,
    While witnesses were filled with strong dismay.

XXIII

THE TRUTH THROUGH GENERATIONS

When the man who formerly had known blindness was
Brought before the Pharisees for questioning,
They could not believe how he had regained his sight;
And they began at once attacking Jesus, declaring,
"This man has broken the Sabbath Law! He can only
Be known as a sinner!" The healed man answered, "Yet,
He opened my eyes." "Are you teaching us, when you
Were born a sinner?" they jeered. And they cast him out.
When Jesus found the man questioned by the Pharisees,
He asked, "Do you believe that the Son of God
Is now speaking to you?" The man then fell to his knees,
As he answered, "My Lord, I believe." And Jesus said,
    "I've come to bring light to the sightless, spiritually,
      And to explain the darkness to those who think they see."

XXIV

PARABLE OF THE GOOD SHEPHERD

Then Jesus said, "The man who does not enter
At the door of the sheepfold, but enters in another way,
Is a thief and a robber; the man who goes by the door
Is recognized as the shepherd exclusively,
So he enters the fold through the gate, since he has become
Their master; he calls each one of his sheep by name
As he leads them out and goes ahead of them.
Because they know his voice, they will follow him."
Then Jesus continued, "I am the door for the sheep,
And whoever comes in by me will be saved, for I
Am their good shepherd, and their safety I will keep,
And for their safety, I'll also be willing to die.

As a shepherd, I know my Father, and He knows me,
And I know each one of my sheep in the very same way

XXV

THE GOOD SAMARITAN

A teacher of the law asked Jesus, "What can I do
To receive eternal life?" And Jesus' reply
Was also a question, "What do the scriptures say?"
"You must love the Lord with all your heart, also
Your fellow man," came the answer. "Do this and you
Will live," said Jesus. "But who is my fellow man?"
And Jesus answered, "On the road to Jericho
A man was attacked by robbers and severely beaten,
And left for dead. A priest then passed him by;
A Levite looked at him, and went his way.
A Samaritan helped him to an inn and agreed to pay
The keeper. As a fellow man which of the three
    Would you choose?" And he said, "The one who was kind."
    And Jesus replied, "Go then, and do the same."

XXVI

DINNER WITH MARTHA AND MARY

When Jesus and His disciples were on their way
To Jerusalem, a woman whose name was Martha
Received Him into her home in Bethany,
And her brother Lazarus and her sister Mary
Were there. Now during the visit, Mary sat
At the Master's feet absorbing each word He was saying,
Until Martha went to Jesus to remonstrate.
"Lord, do you not care that all of the serving
Has been left to me by my sister? Tell her, then
To help me!" But the Lord replied to the worrisome Martha,
"Why are you troubled over many things, when
In truth, one thing only is needed as mainstay?

    Mary has chosen that which will always endure,
    And it shall never be taken away from her."

XXVII

JESUS SETS OUT FOR JERUSALEM

Near the time of Passover they were on the road
Going up to Jerusalem, with Jesus walking
Ahead of His disciples, and they were afraid;
As they looked at the figure of Jesus, there seemed to be something
About Him which make them hesitate to intrude
Upon His loneliness. At last He took
The twelve aside to a place away from the road,
To prepare them for what He knew was ahead. He spoke,
"All that is written about the Son of Man
Will come true, He'll be handed over to the teachers of law
To be condemned to death, and handed over again
To the Gentiles who will whip Him, mock Him and finally
    They will kill Him, but after three days He will rise to life."
    The disciples listened, but could not conceive of His strife.

XXVIII

THE PRODIGAL SON

While east of the Jordan, Jesus spoke in a parable
To His disciples. "A man had two sons and the younger
One said to him, "Father, would you enable
Me to leave by giving me my share
Of holdings that falls to me?" And obligingly,
The father divided the estate, and the son was soon
On a journey afar where he squandered his property,
Until famine arose in the land and he began
To be in want. Then he said, "I'll go to my father
And seek forgiveness, and ask to be his hired
Servant." But his father ran to meet the traveler,
And embraced him, and turning to his older son, he said,

    "It is fitting to make merry and allow our joy to abound,
    For your brother who was dead is alive; he was lost,
    and is found."

XXIX

DEATH OF LAZARUS

A man named Lazarus who lived in Bethany
Became ill. It was in Bethany where Martha
And her sister Mary lived, the very same Mary
Who sat and listened to Jesus on many a day.
Now these two sisters sent word to Jesus, saying,
"Our brother is ill," At the time when Jesus received
The message, He said, "The result of this happening
Will not be Lazarus' death for this unrelieved
Illness will be the means of revealing God's glory."
And two days later when Jesus went back to Judea,
He was met by the saddened words of the sister Martha,
"If you had been here, we would never have received this blow."
    And Jesus replied, "Whosoever believes in me
    Will live, for those who believe shall never die."

XXX

THE RESURRECTION OF LAZARUS

And when Jesus saw Mary weeping for her brother, He
Was deeply moved, and He went to the tomb and said
To the mourners there, "Take the stone away."
But Martha, the older sister, then demurred,
"Lord! It has been four days since he was buried."
And Jesus said to her, "Didn't I tell you
That your brother, Lazarus, will never be dead?"
It was then that the people rolled the stone away
While Jesus raised his eyes and prayed, "Father,
Thank you!" A pause, then, "Lazarus, I say
Come out." And the man appeared in his grave attire.
"Untie him," Jesus told them, "and let him go."

    From that day onward, those in authority
    Made plans to kill Jesus, so He traveled judiciously.

XXXI

JESUS BLESSES LITTLE CHILDREN

With a sense of urgency then Jesus withdrew
To the region near where He had been baptized
Several years before; and because of what He knew
Concerning His remaining time, He summarized
The qualities which make for eternal life.
As Jesus spoke, mothers with little children
Were asking Him for prayers on their behalf,
But they were being resisted by Peter and John,
Until Jesus said, "Let the little children come
To me, for of such is the Kingdom of Heaven, and when
There is one who fails to receive the Heavenly Kingdom
As a little child, he shall never enter therein."

    Then Jesus bade the children draw near to Him,
    And He touched the head of each in blessing them.

XXXII

ZACCHAEUS MEETS JESUS

As Jesus was making His way through Jericho,
The chief collector of taxes named Zacchaeus,
Well known for his smallness of stature, was determined to see
The Master, so he ran ahead of the crowd and was ingenious
Enough to climb the tallest sycamore tree,
The better to view the Lord as the passerby.
When Jesus looked up in the tree, He said, "Hurry
Down, Zacchaeus, I'd like to stay
At your place today." And Jesus went to his home,
Where he said, "I'll give half my belongings to the poor,
And if I've cheated anyone, I'll pay him
Back four times." And Jesus answered, I'm sure
    That true salvation has come to this house today,
    For the Son of Man seeks those who have lost their way."

XXXIII

ARE YOU THE MESSIAH?

The time had come to celebrate the Feast
Of Dedication in Jerusalem; it was winter
And on Solomon's porch they were saying, "Tell us, at last,
Are you the Messiah whom we seek? Give us your answer
Now." And Jesus said, "I've told you already,
My sheep all listen to my voice and follow
Me to life eternal, for they shall never die.
What my Father has given me, no one can snatch away
From His loving care, for my Father and I are together
As one." Once more they picked up stones to throw
At Jesus, and He said to them, "My good works are before
You. For which of these do you wish to stone me?"
   And they answered, "You insult God! You're only a man."
   But before they could arrest Him, He escaped across the
   Kidron.

SONG OF THE SON OF MAN

The Final Days in the Earthly Ministry of Jesus Christ

BOOK III
OF A
TRILOGY

I

LOVE'S EXTRAVAGANCE

At the time of Passover then Jesus went
To dine with Lazarus whom He'd raised from the dead;
And as Martha was serving, Mary took a pint
Of nard and anointed Jesus' feet and spread
Her hair to dry them while fragrance was everywhere.
Then Judas, planning betrayal, protested and said,
"The poor could have gained from the sale of a product so rare."
Though in truth it was he who often profited.
"Let her observe this event knowing no reprieve,"
Said Jesus, "You'll not have me with you always,
But Mary's lovely deed, fulfilled on this eve
Of Passover exceeding all yesterdays,
    This memory of love which knows no measure,
      Shall ever remain the world's most precious treasure."

II

JERUSALEM ENTRY

He knew of His peril when He paused on Olivet
And viewed the valley where pilgrims were journeying
To Jerusalem. And His heart cried out, "Oh yet,
Like a mother hen would I gather you under my wing!
But when ears are closed then eyes must be made to see."
Then Jesus turned to the colt of a donkey as planned,
And rode upon its back as He entered the valley
To the greetings of waving palms as He approached
The Golden Gate. With arms outstretched, He was saying,
With the prophets, "Fear not! Behold your king!" But the claim
Was made from the beast of peace in offering,
And not from the horse of war, when Jesus came.
 It was thus He made His claim and His last appeal
 For open hearts to God's own commonweal.

III

CLEANSING THE TEMPLE

When Jesus entered the city on Monday morning
He went directly to the temple where the previous night's
Scene was etched upon His mind as a huckstering
Marketplace at the Court of the Israelites.
In anger He viewed the changers of money exacting their fee
For purchase of sacrifice, while setting a ban
Upon all else, thus making mockery
Of the offer of the heart of love to God, and to man.
"My house of prayer has become a den of thieves,"
He cried. But His action was not as one dealing with abuse
Of thieves at money tables and of sellers of doves,
But as God who was sweeping evil from His house.

    Though Jesus saw the danger, He could not have withdrawn,
    For He'd burned His bridges, in crossing His Rubicon.

IV

THE POWER OF FAITH

On Tuesday when Jesus and His twelve were on their way
To the city, they saw the tree where He had scratched
For figs. "The tree has withered since yesterday."
Said Peter. "And so it shall be," the Master answered,
"When it's not bearing. But bid the mountains depart,
And if your faith is strong, and you truly believe
In what you are asking within your heart,
Then God will hear your prayer, and you shall receive.
And when you pray, ask yourself if you
Are harboring evil thoughts of wrathfulness;
For if you are, absolve and start anew,
That your Father may then forgive your trespasses.
    For it's true that God can do no more for men,
    Than they would do for any citizen."

V

BY WHAT AUTHORITY?

When Jesus walked in the temple courts that day
The priests and scribes then came to Him and said,
"By what authority did you drive away
The merchants yesterday?" And Jesus replied,
"If you will answer me, then I'll answer you,
Was John God's messenger, or indeed, a seditious
Man?" They reasoned among themselves, "It is true,
The people will be angered if we say he was vicious,
And if we claim him as a prophet, then they will ask,
"But how could it happen that you did not believe?"
Then Jesus spake, "If you will not unmask
Your belief, I'll not reveal how I receive."

So for those who failed to speak the truth, the way
Was blocked, until there was nothing more to say.

VI

THE GREATEST COMMANDMENT

On the floor of the temple a scribe came forth and said,
"Oh Lord, you surely speak as God's own son.
Now which is the greatest commandment?" And Jesus answered
Him, "Hear this, the Lord our God is one,
You shall love the Lord with all your heart and soul,
And with all your mind. A commandment which I call
The second is this, 'Love your neighbor,' and of the whole
Of the ten, these two are the greatest of them all."
The scribe replied, "I give witness that you speak
The truth, for love transcends all offerings too."
And Jesus said to him, "That which you seek
Is found, for the Kingdom of God is now in you:

    For all on earth who seek the way above
    Shall be as one in Convenant of Love."

VII

A KERNEL OF WHEAT

Among the Passover guests were certain astute
Men who questioned Jesus, and He said, "If a kernel
Of wheat shall die in the ground it bringeth fruit,
For he who loses his life shall find it eternal.
Shall I ask to be saved from this hour? But for this cause
I came." And from the heavens a voice was saying,
"You are glorified!" And Jesus continued, "Because
I'll draw all men when I'm lifted." Thus signifying
His death. And they asked, "We've heard that Christ abideth
Always. Who is this one to be at the right
Of God?" And Jesus answered, "He that walketh
In darkness sees nothing; be children of light."

 A hush then fell upon all who'd make suggestions,
 And after that, none dared to ask more questions.

VIII

THE WICKED HUSBANDMEN

Then Jesus began to speak in a parable;
"A man once planted a vineyard and discouraged marauding
By surrounding it with hedge to make it stable;
Then he left it until the time of harvesting.
And when the abundant fruit was ripe in his vineyard,
The owner sent a servant to collect from his unlanded
Tenants who held his trust in disregard,
And the messenger was sent away empty-handed.
When a second came, they killed him and many others
Until the owner sent his beloved son,
Who was also thrown out by the wicked harvesters.
Now the owner will come, and the evil shall be undone."

    Thus ended the day of questioning on the floor
    Of the temple, and Jesus left, to return no more.

IX

JUDAS PLOTS

At the time when priests and scribes were secretly
Meeting with Ciaphas to plan a stratagem
For seizing and holding the Lord in custody,
One of the twelve arrived to plot with them.
He was Judas Iscariot who sought to convey
A plan. "And what would you pay?" asked the bargainer,
"For I know the very hour in which to betray
Him." They agreed that thirty pieces of silver
Would be his price and Judas reasoned that surely
No harm could come from the meeting, and furthermore
If it all should bring about an emergency,
Then the Master could disappear as He'd done before.
    So the signal was set, and all were in accord
    That the kiss of Judas would identify the Lord.

X

PREPARATION FOR PASSOVER

Then came the day of the feast of Unleavened Bread,
And the sacrifice of the lamb at Passover,
When Jesus called His twelve to Him and said,
"On God's own day we'll eat the Paschal supper
Alone." And then He turned to John and Peter
And said, "In the city you'll find one carrying
A pitcher of water. Let him know the Teacher
Says, 'My time is at hand. This evening
We'll keep the Passover in a certain household.'
You'll be shown an upper room for company."
The disciples went and found it all as told,
And at the hour, Jesus sat and convivially
    Began the blessed meal which came to be
    Shared by hungering humanity.

XI

HUMILITY

At the feast of Passover He heard the dissent
Of His twelve as to who'd be greatest in the new kingdom.
Then Jesus girded Himself with towel and bent
To wash His disciples' feet midst shamed and awesome
Hush, until He came to Peter's side.
"Lord, why dost thou wash my feet?" he enquired.
And Jesus said, "Thou shalt know, but now abide."
"Master! You'll never wash my feet," he declared.
"If I wash thee not, thou hast no part with me."
Came the grave reply. "Then wash my hands and head,"
He cried, "Since thou art clean, that need not be."
When again in robe and at feast with twelve, He said,
     "You call me Lord, and rightly so, it's true,
     Then you should do as I have done for you."

XII

DISMISSAL OF JUDAS

In tender fellowship with the twelve on night
Of feast it was known to Jesus irrevocably,
He must cast from vine a branch long lost in blight.
He spoke, "One of you will soon betray me."
In disbelief, then each one shook his head.
"Who is it, Lord?" And Jesus said, "It's the one who
Shall receive this sop." And then He gave the bread
To Judas, saying, "Do what you must do."
When Judas went out with the bag, the disciples thought
He'd been asked to purchase against the needs of the morrow;
And yet a sudden strangeness in Iscariot
Held all in upper room in silent sorrow,

 As Judas went into darkest night to fulfill
 His evil mission which was darker still.

XIII

THE LORD'S SUPPER (THE BREAD)

In the hush of the upper room, then Jesus said,
"I've long desired to eat this Passover with you."
And then He took a loaf of bread and blessed it,
Saying, "The true Bread comes down from my Father
In heaven, and gives life to the world. And I say again,
As I've said before, I am the Bread of life,
And those who come to me shall know no pain
Of hunger, nor shall they thirst. As I break this loaf
So shall my body be broken, a testament
To the truth. And now may each of you partake
Of this most blessed Paschal sacrament,
The supper of the Lord, for memories sake,
  For the Bread of the crucified Son of Man shall be
  The life of your soul, throughout eternity"

XIV

THE LORD'S SUPPER (THE CUP)

And at table after supper, Jesus likewise
Sat with His disciples and took a cup, And when
He'd blessed it, He said, "This cup doth symbolize
The life which I shall give unto all men.
It's the covenant in my blood, poured out to sustain
The many who seek the grace of the comforter.
Now share it, for I'll not drink of it again
Until I'm in the kingdom of my Father.
Henceforth, as often as you shall break the bread
And drink, you proclaim the death of the Lord for you;
For he who eats my flesh and drinks my blood
Abides in me, as I'm in him anew,

    And every common meal is both remembrance,
    And witness of my everlasting presence."

XV

PETER'S DENIAL FORETOLD

As Jesus and His eleven were at table together,
He said, "This night you'll all be offended by me,
For it's written, 'I'll smite the shepherd and the sheep will scatter.'
But when I'm risen, I'll go into Galilee."
Then Peter exclaimed, "If they all fall away this night
I'll never leave you." And Jesus answered, "It's true
That Satan's made a strong demand that he might
Take you, and like small grains of wheat to sift you,
However, I long have prayed that your faith may never
Falter, and you'll turn to strengthen your brethren." "But I'll go
With you," cried Peter, "even as a prisoner."
Came the answer, "You'll deny me thrice ere cock shall crow."
    But Peter persisted, "I'll never deny your name,"
    While all of the other apostles said the same.

XVI

FAREWELL

"Though I'm with you a little while," said Jesus to His sorrowing
Disciples, "Let not your heart be troubled. You believe
In God. My Father's house has many dwelling
Places. I'll go, but I'll come again to receive
You. . . And you know the way I'm going." In dubious
Tones, spoke Thomas, "How can we know the way?"
"I am the way, the truth, and the life," said Jesus
"In me you've known my Father, to whom I pray.
But I'll not go and leave you comfortless;
I'll come again, and I shall pray my Father
To send the Holy Spirit, in graciousness
To lead to truth and to abide with you forever.

    And now, I give you a peace forever true;
     It's not of the world; it's my peace I give to you."

XVII

THE VINE AND THE BRANCHES

And when they'd sung a hymn, His faithful eleven
With Jesus left upper room and went out of the city
To seek a familiar path across the Kedron
Channel to the garden of Gethsemane.
And Jesus talked as they walked beneath the sheltering
Trees. "I am the vine and my Father the Vinedresser.
And when He finds a branch which is harvesting
No fruit, He prunes the branches for a greater
Yield. You are clean through the words I've spoken already,
And just as the branch can bear no fruit unless
It grows in the vine, you must also abide in me,
For I am the vine, and you are the branches.
    A last commandment I leave as I go to my Father:
    As I have loved you, you shall also love one another."

XVIII

INTERCESSORY PRAYER

At the garden Jesus lifted His eyes to heaven
And said, "Oh, Father, the hour has come. Thou did'st grant
Eternal life to all whom Thou hast given
To thy son through knowing the Christ whom Thou hast sent.
And have lost but one that the scriptures read the same.
I've made known Thy name unto these men of mine,
As Thou sent me, I send out these men of thine,
And I pray Thou shalt keep them always in thy name.
I pray for those who come to believe in me
Through their word; may thy love which I have known,
Oh Father, sustain and keep them as one, even as we,
That the truth may dwell throughout the earth, forever.
    Oh, Holy Father, we've walked the world as one
    Now grant me thy presence as before the world was begun."

XIX

AGONY IN GETHSEMANE

At the time of darkest night in Gethsemane,
When Jesus knew His hour was drawing near,
He walked with Peter, and the sons of Zebedee
In deepening pain. And He said, "Tarry here
And watch with me." He prayed as He knelt upon
The ground, "Remove this cup, nevertheless,
Thy will be done." And when Peter, James and John
Were found asleep, He spoke in loneliness.
"Could you not watch one hour? It's for your sake
I've prayed. The spirit is willing, but the flesh is weak."
A second time He found no friend awake;
On His third return the three heard Him speak,

    "Awake! The hour of darkness now has come,
    Through God's own will to move the pendulum."

XX

THE ARREST

When the band of high priest's soldiers made loud the night
In the garden, with Judas in the lead, they saw
The figure of Jesus step forth into the light
Asking, "Whom do you seek?" And the soldiers, in awe
Fell back, but as Judas greeted the Master, He asked,
"Would you betray the Son of Man with a kiss?"
Then Peter drew forth his sword in his bold and spirited
Manner, and cut off the ear of a slave of Ananias.
But Jesus caused it to heal while admonishing
Simon, "He who lives by the sword must also die by it."
He turned to the soldiers. "It's your hour we are witnessing."
And they seized the Lord, and led Him from the moonlit
    Garden, while His disciples forsook Him and fled,
    Until two faced about, and followed instead.

XXI

PETER'S DENIAL

He entered high priest's palace gate
And joined with those round brazier's welcome glow!
He'd followed close to learn of Jesus' fate,
But Peter's heart had warned, he well did know.
Soon spoke an officer, close by his side,
"In truth wasn't thou with Him of Galilee?"
"I do not know the man," Peter denied.
A maid affirmed, "Thou knowst Gethsemane."
"Not true," was his reply. "He's one of them!"
A third accused. With Peter's quick, "Not so!"
Came crow of cock and Jesus' words to him,
"Thou shalt deny me thrice, ere cock shall crow."

    Consumed in pain by vows he had not kept,
    'Twas bitterly, he bowed his head and wept.

XXII

ANANIAS AND JESUS

The judge and the prisoner were in striking tableau;
The aged priest, and the One with His claim divine.
With Ananias seated on the portico
Of his palace, while before him was the bane of Palestine.
As the priest considered the man whose basic tenet
Was love, he knew the view could pose no danger.
But of late, the people were leaving temple, and when it
Was known He was near, all followed this one to the manger
Born, and at once to beset Him with pleas for healing.
But he'd not try the man; let Ciaphas address
Himself to that . . . and yet, were it not festering
Temple cleansing, it could be less merciless.

    The old priest stood and drew erect his frame,
    To order that Jesus be sent to face the blame

XXIII

SANHEDRIN TRIAL

Then Jesus faced the court of the Great Sanhedrin
With its chairs facing marble walls on either side
Now being filled with elders who'd soon be sitting in
Judgment of the summary which justified
The formal charting of the path to Golgotha.
In private meeting the charge of blasphemy
Had come from doubts of His claim to being the Messiah,
When His answer, "I am," rang out, unequivocally . . .
The spirit of the court was broken in the witnesseth,
No rights were conserved, but systematically
Destroyed as authorities joined to compass death
Of Jesus who knew the outcome before their decree.
    He also knew that with all of man's deceit,
    The purpose of God could not be brought to defeat.

XXIV

JUDAS REPENTS

A new feeling had come to Judas as he watched them leading
Jesus to the Courtroom near the Pool of Siloe.
His feeling came not from friendship, but from an acceding
To utter goodness of the man he'd come to know.
He rushed to the priests to reverse his villainy.
"It's wrong to betray His innocent blood," he cried.
"What's that to us?" said the priests, indifferently,
As they heard the ring of dancing silver while wildeyed
Judas made way to the Gate of Bethlehem.
And outside the city wall where he climbed to the top
Of a tree which hung over the valley of Hinnon.
When his neck was secured, there came the sound of a snap,
    And his body lay sprawled on the rocks below the fig,
    Like a marionette attached to its fruitless twig.

XXV

BEFORE PILATE

"Take Him and try Him yourselves," cried the Procurator
As he turned from the mob, and walked from the balcony
To his quarters within, where Caesar's Administrator
Then sent for the prisoner to offer His plea.
When Jesus entered, Pilate went to His side.
"Your kingdom?" he asked. "It's not a worldly one,"
Said Jesus. "Then you *are* a king!" he cried.
"I testify to the truth as my Father's Son."
"And what is the truth?" snapped Pilate, moving to appear
Again on the balcony in the judgment seat.
"Not guilty!" he said. "Galilee, now hear!"
They were shouting as he grasped the changing balance sheet.

    "This properly is not a case for me.
    You must take Him to Herod, Tetrarch of Galilee."

XXVI

TO HEROD

As his father was haunted by murder, King Herod's spector
Was the life of John the Baptist for whom he'd shown
No mercy when Salome had requested his head as a favor
For a dance. With Jesus he could perhaps atone
For his wrong. So he ordered that the cousin of John be allowed
To enter. He rose in the greeting, a willing avower
Of Jesus' fame, and as king he would be proud
To witness some display of that special power
Well known as symbol of Jesus' ministry.
Perhaps some miracle which had gained acclaim?
But the silence was affront to Herod's dignity,
And as comic king He was ordered to whence He came.
    Thus Pilate's deference to Herod on that bitter day
    Served only the infamous journey to delay.

XXVII

TO PILATE AGAIN

Word was received at the fortress Antonia
That Herod had found no crime in the witnessing;
But as Pilate noted the paraphernalia
Of Jesus' attire denoting a spurious king
In mockery, he said, accordingly,
"I detect no guilt in Him, for He's done nothing
To deserve the way of the cross in penalty."
Then came a burst of venom so shattering
That the startled governor became aware
Of the demand for pardon of the prisoner Barabbas.
"And Jesus?" he asked, as anger filled the air.
"To the cross," came the cry, and to end the habeas,
 He ordered the prisoner to "half way death,"
 Where the thread of life is held in a single breath.

XXVIII

CONDEMNED

When the soldiers led Jesus away from the scourging
He was taken to Pilate in His terrible finery
Of tattered robe, His body bruised with the purging
To satisfy the mob sufficiently
To set Him free. When again before the Sanhedrin
Men, then Pilate turned and spoke from the judgment
Seat. "Behold! I find no fault in Him."
"To the cross! Away with Him!" came the angry chant.
And Pilate asked, "Shall I crucify your king?"
"We have no king but Caesar," from the countryside
Came the answer which left no space for arguing.
Defeated . . .he gave Jesus to be crucified.

    To thwart the mob, he'd presented a king uncouth,
    While in that gesture was everlasting truth.

XXIX

THE QUARTERNION

A bitter Pilate called the Centurian
Abenadar, and ordered that a sign be made
Proclaiming a king, and in keeping with the plan
At the top of the Cross the sign should be displayed.
Now Abenadar was aware of the requisition
Items: from soldiers to crucifixion trees which he'd
Need in the task of arranging the regulation
Quarternion, with a calvaryman in the lead.
When the column was formed, he walked the length of it,
And with all in order, he called a forward march,
While high priests drew themselves aside to permit
The parade a passage through Antonia's arch.

    And the steps were taken which history
    Shall live forever in their infamy.

XXX

TO THE CROSS

The procession from Antonia to the hill
Was through narrow streets with houses crowded close on
Either side. At the spot where Jesus fell
The centurian ordered a stranger to assume His burden.
It was Simon of Cyrene, forever honored for his aid
To Jesus. When all pressed on, the throng which followed them
Grew larger with number of women who bewailed and lamented,
Until Jesus stopped. "Oh daughters of Jerusalem,
Weep not for me," He said, "Because the day
Will come when they will say, 'How happy the breasts
Which will never feed a child!' They will also say
To the mountains, and to the hills, 'Oh fall on us.'"

    But then Abenadar came back to restrain
    The talk, and the marchers started up again.

XXXI

FATHER, FORGIVE THEM

When they came to the "Place of the Skull" the barren-spirited
Soldiers drove long nails through His hands to the wood
Of the cross. And then when He refused the wine the deathshead
Beam was raised in the socket, while some who stood
Below looking up at Jesus, in mockery
Cried out, "Oh, Thou, who'd render the temple asunder,
And then within three days so brilliantly
Would raise it up again, now where's your power,
Oh king? Come down and save yourself!" And then Jesus
Gazed at the jeering crowd with eyes that grew
More sad, until He prayed from the depths of His bounteous
Love, "Forgive them Father for they know not what they do."
     And in that prayer which rose from searing pain
     Was promise that all may yet be born again.

XXXII

YOU'LL BE WITH ME IN PARADISE

And when the crosses of each of the thieves were jolted
Into the ground at Jesus' either side,
They too joined in the blasphemy while tortured
By their pain, until one turned to chide
His fellow brigand, "Do you have no fear of God?"
He asked. "We also are condemned, and for this
We now receive our true and just reward,
But we know this man had done no deed amiss."
And then he said to Jesus, "Remember me
In your kingdom." And Jesus answered, "Though men despise
You, I say your faith has set you free.
For today, you'll be with me in Paradise." So while numbered
 Among the transgressors, He made a place
 For all who repent and seek the gift of God's grace.

XXXIII

BEHOLD THY MOTHER

He saw the soldiers below the cross then lift
A part of His clothing, and spread it flat for a better
View of His outer garment, a precious gift
Of His mother, when He'd gone out to the world on another
Day. With the sound of rolling dice, His thoughts
Were of scripture words, "They parted my garments among them,
And for my rainment, they then did cast their lots."
He looked away from the soldiers, not to condemn
Their action, but tenderly to view the one
Who was standing so close to the cross with John, His ever
Loving mother. He said, "Behold thy mother!"

    For His heart had been held in human bonds as He'd trod
    The earthly ways, to His ultimate oneness with God.

XXXIV

FORSAKEN?

It happened at the end of the morning on Golgotha
And caused all insults hurled at the Nazarene
To come to a sudden halt, as the phenomena
Of midnight darkness settled on the noonday scene
Of the crucifixion. It was as if the sun
Had spent itself and could no longer bear
To look upon the deed man's hand had done,
And a deepening silence settled everywhere.
Some left the hill, while others hovered in the darkness
Of that awesome afternoon, until nearly three
O'clock, when Jesus seemed most comfortless,
As He cried, "Oh why hast Thou forsaken me?"
    For in plumbing the depths of the human condition,
    The Son of Man was completing His earthly mission.

XXXV

I THIRST

Again from the unfathomable depths of His seeming despair,
There came a second agonized outburst
From Jesus, as parched by the torture of hanging there
Upon the cross, He then cried out, "I thirst!"
For He was all of God and all of man,
And in those hours of pain, He'd humanly
Suffered a thirst, as with the Samaritan
At Jacob's well, on His way to Galilee.
When soured wine was offered below His feet,
To His mind came the words of the one who was able to forethink
The crucifixion. "They gave me gall for meat;
And in my thirst they gave vinegar to drink."
    But He knew that the nard poured out n Bethany,
    Was extravagance for all humanity.

XXXVI

IT'S FINISHED

At three o'clock a light outlined Him there
Upon the cross, and as the soldiers offered
Soured wine to ease His thirst, the air
Was filled with His tremendous shout, "It's finished!"
And at that moment, in full reality,
Life's events were before the inward eye of Jesus,
And revealed in each part of their totality
He found full measure in all that had come to pass;
For even as God had created the heaven and earth,
And all that is held within, and could say, "It's done,"
So Jesus knew that His mission from the time of His birth
Was held in the words, "Thou art my beloved Son."
    And the Father could call His finished creation good,
    In its final casting with the bonds of Brotherhood.

XXXVII

INTO THY HANDS I COMMIT MY SPIRIT

Through the echo of Jesus' loud outcry, a glory
Streamed around the cross with the brilliance of sunlit
Day, as He prayed to all eternity,
"Father, into Thy hands, I commit my spirit."
When His head fell forward, no sound was heard from below,
As He silently breathed His last . . . but at that moment
Came a quaking of earth sending boulders to and fro,
And the temple veil of the Holy of Holies was rent
In twain, as the way to the very presence of the Father,
Then known to few, was open to all, through Jesus,
Who removed the veil, allowing mortals as never
Before, to view the love of God on the Cross:
    And the centurion, kneeling in wonder upon the sod,
    Pronounced, "He surely was the Son of God."

XXXVIII

THE BURIAL

With the crucifixion task at last completed,
Then Joseph of Arimathea went straightway
To Pilate to claim the body of the Lord
For the purpose of burial on Preparation Day.
Now near the Cross was a garden plot
With sepulchre wherein no one yet laid;
And Nichodemus gave aid in removing to the spot
The body of Jesus for burial in the newmade
Grave. The body was prepared for burying
While the Marys lingered near the tomb where He lay,
Until a stone had closed its opening,
When they hurried homeward to keep the Sabbath Day.
    And as darkness began to settle, all was still
    At the grave near the three empty trees that marked the hill.

XXXIX

SILENT WATCH

On this day that spelled the time of Preparation
The priests approached the Governor to obtain
Permission. "Sir," they said, "In defraudation,
The deceiver has said, 'Three days and I'll rise again!'
So we ask that a guard be placed at the tomb and continued
Three days, lest during the Sabbatical
They steal the body and say, 'He's risen from the dead!'
Making this deception worse than the original."
And Pilate answered, "Your plan I shall condone;
Now go and make it all as secure as you can."
So the opening of the tomb was sealed with a stone,
And a watch was kept by appointed custodians
    Of the cave wherein the Man of Galilee
    Was lovingly laid to rest from Calvary.

XL

HE'S RISEN

Arriving in the garden before the watch was over.
The women saw the stone rolled away from the tomb.
Then Mary ran until she met John and Peter. "He's gone!"
She cried. "And we don't know where they've laid Him."
The two disciples reached the tomb apart
From Mary, and finding the grave clothes still in their folds,
It was John who understood, while Peter's heart
Was troubled as the two returned to their households.
But Mary stood weeping beside the heavy stone
When a voice said, "Mary." And she answered, "Master!"
"Tell them," He said, "And I'll seek Peter alone!"
And Mary went with the words, "I've seen the Lord!"
    On that Holy Morn the Great Interpreter
    Was Love, revealing the living Christ, forever.

XLI

WALK TO EMMAUS

On that day two men were on their way
To the village of Emmaus, not far from the Holy City,
And as they talked about the event of the day,
They remained oblivious to the proximity
Of Jesus as He journeyed with them, until finally
He spoke to the two, "Why is your conversation
So troubled as you walk along?" In temerity
Both men stood still. "Are you the only one
Who hasn't heard about Jesus of Nazareth?"
They asked. And Jesus answered, "How slow you are
To believe the Messiah has suffered to conquer death."
On that night, His talking was like a fire
    In them, and when He broke the bread, they agreed
    At once with the news, "This is the Lord, indeed."

XLII

WITH HIS TEN

The men who'd been with Jesus in Emmaus went back
To Jerusalem to tell the disciples about walking
With Him, and how they'd recognized Him as He broke
The bread at the evening meal. While the two were telling
Their news, the Lord appeared and stood with them,
Saying, "Peace be with you," and noting their fear
He asked, "Why are you troubled? This is my time
To show myself." And they were filled with wonder
As He talked, and opened their eyes to the scriptures, saying,
"The Messiah must suffer in helping others to forgive. Let His
Message of repentance be preached to all nations, beginning
In Jerusalem, where you'll wait for the power from above

    To come upon you. Again, I say, "Peace be
    With you," as the Father sent me, I now send you."

XLIII

JESUS AND THOMAS

One of the twelve disciples, called the twin,
Was not with the ten when Jesus came, so the other
Disciples told him, "We saw the Lord!" And then,
Thomas expressed his doubts. "It will not be clear
To me that the Master lives," he said to them,
"Unless I see His scars I cannot conceive
The wonderment that we shall ever have Him
With us. When I can touch Him, then I'll believe."
Later, when the disciples were all together again,
The doors were locked, and Jesus came and stood
Near Thomas and said, "Put your hand in my side." It was then
That Thomas answered Him, "My Lord, and my God!"
    And Jesus said, "So now you are able to see me.
    How happy are those who believe, but do not see."

XLIV

JESUS AND FIVE FISHERMEN

Later, Jesus revealed Himself to several
Of His apostles at the Sea of Galilee,
Where it happened that Peter, Thomas and Nathaniel,
With James and John had fished all night, when they saw
Someone on the beach. "Cast to the right."
He called. And when they did so, their nets were full.
John looked at Peter, "It's the Lord!" he said. But
They could not be sure, until a short time later,
When they beached the boat and saw a charcoal fire,
With fish being broiled over it, and bread. And when Peter
Had hauled the large catch ashore, they heard the
Words, "Come and have breakfast." Which were said.

And though they'd recognized Jesus by that time,
They ate in silence the fish which He served to them.

XLV

JESUS AND PETER

After they'd eaten, Jesus said to Peter,
"Simon, son of John, do you love me more
Than these?" And Simon Peter was quick to answer,
"Yes, Lord, I love you." And Jesus said, "Then care
For my lambs." And then, again Jesus asked,
"Simon Peter! Do you truly love me?"
"You know I love you," answered Peter, sorrowed
Deeply by Jesus' second inquiry.
And Jesus said, "Take care of my sheep." . . . A third
Time, then Jesus asked, "Simon, son
Of John, do you love me?" And Peter demurred,
"You know all things. You know I love you." And then
    The answer, "Feed my sheep! Admittedly
     You'll encounter suffering, but follow me."

XLVI

ASCENSION

For forty days after His crucifixion
Jesus showed Himself to His disciples many
Times, and His teachings were designed to keep them attune
To His mission both humanly and spiritually.
"Wait in Jerusalem until my Father
Has given you the gift which will befit
Your purpose," He said. "John baptized with water,
But shortly you will be baptized with the Holy Spirit."
Then He led them out to Bethany,
Where He lifted up His hands at last and blessed them
And His blessing held them in feelings of rhapsody
As He parted from them and was taken to His home in heaven.
    And when His disciples returned to Jerusalem,
    They spent their time in the temple, worshipping Him.

POSTLUDE

XLVII

PENTECOST

The disciples were together at time of Pentecost
When the sound of wind came to where they were staying
And tongues of fire which touched their shoulders unloosed
Their tongues in languages outrivaling their own.
In the Holy City some Jews were staying;
Men devout who came from a multitude
Of nations, who marveled, "These Galileans are speaking
In our very own tongues of the mighty works of God!"
Then Peter stood before them and lifted his voice;
"We are witnesses that Jesus was raised to abide
At His Father's right hand, and He'd received His promise
Of the Holy Spirit with which we're now sanctified.

    That His story be told, until nations with one accord
    Ring out in praise of Jesus Christ, our Lord!"

If my readers share even one half of the joy which I have experienced during this journey, then indeed, it will have been worthwhile.

Elizabeth Newell Berglund